Editor   Karen Barker
Language Consultant   Betty Root
Natural History Consultant   Dr Gerald Legg

Carolyn Scrace is a graduate of Brighton College of Art, specialising in design and illustration. She has worked in animation, advertising and children's fiction and non-fiction. She is a major contributor to the popular *Worldwise* series and *The X-ray Picture Book* series, particularly **Amazing Animals**, **Your Body** and **Dinosaurs**.

Betty Root was the Director of the Reading and Language Information Centre at the University of Reading for over twenty years. She has worked on numerous children's books, both fiction and non-fiction, and has also held the position of Smarties Book Award Judge.

Dr Gerald Legg holds a doctorate in zoology from Manchester University. His current position is biologist at the Booth Museum of Natural History in Brighton.

David Salariya was born in Dundee, Scotland, where he studied illustration and printmaking, concentrating on book design in his post-graduate year. He has designed and created many new series of children's books for publishers in the U.K. and overseas.

Printed in Belgium.   J181,767   €10

An SBC Book conceived, edited and designed by
The Salariya Book Company
25 Marlborough Place, Brighton BN1 1UB

©The Salariya Book Company Ltd MCMXCVIII

A CIP catalogue record for this book is available from the British Library

ISBN 0 7496 5034 6

This edition 2003
First published in Great Britain in 1999 by
Franklin Watts
96 Leonard Street
London
EC2A 4XD

Franklin Watts Australia
45-51 Huntley Street
Alexandria
NSW 2015

lifecycles

The Journey of a Turtle

Written and Illustrated by Carolyn Scrace

Created and Designed by David Salariya

W
FRANKLIN WATTS
LONDON • SYDNEY

Green turtles live in warm seas.
They swim long distances
to islands in the
Atlantic and Pacific Oceans
(see map on pages 26-27).
There they lay their eggs
on sandy beaches.
Afterwards the turtles
swim home again.
Their whole journey is called
a *migration*.
In this book you can follow the
amazing migration of a green turtle.

Green turtles are
covered by a large
horny shell.
They have
two strong
front flippers,
which they use like paddles
when they swim.

Horny shell

Strong front
flippers

Adult green turtles
eat plants such as seaweed.
They find their food in shallow water.

The turtles
leave their feeding grounds
when the weather gets colder,
and start to migrate.
They are strong swimmers.
Some turtles swim over
2,500 kilometres for
their migration journey.

The turtles reach the breeding ground.
The female turtle waits until nightfall
then drags herself up the beach.
She uses her flippers to dig a hole
called a nesting chamber.
This is where she lays
her eggs.

Nesting chamber

The female turtle comes onto the beach at night because the sand is cooler then. Other animals cannot see her in the dark, so it is safer too.

The female turtle lays over 100 eggs
in the nesting chamber.
She pushes sand over the hole
to hide the eggs.

After about ten days
the turtle returns
to lay a new clutch of eggs
in another nesting chamber.
During about two months she lays
five or six clutches of eggs.

When dawn comes
the female turtle
drags herself back
down the beach.
She swims out to sea,
where the male turtle
is waiting for her.

The male and
female turtle mate.

The sand covering the nest
protects the eggs from
the heat of the sun.
Inside the eggs,
baby turtles begin to grow.

J181,767   21

After about 7 weeks the baby turtles start to hatch. At nightfall, the baby turtles dig themselves out of the nesting hole and crawl down the beach to the sea.

Crabs, birds, snakes and cats will all try to eat baby turtles on land. In the sea they can be eaten by sharks and crocodiles.

Once they reach the sea,
the baby turtles start their
long journey back
to the feeding ground.

The parent turtles do not
wait for them and not all of
the baby turtles will survive.

The parents
and young turtles
who do get home
have completed
the migration.

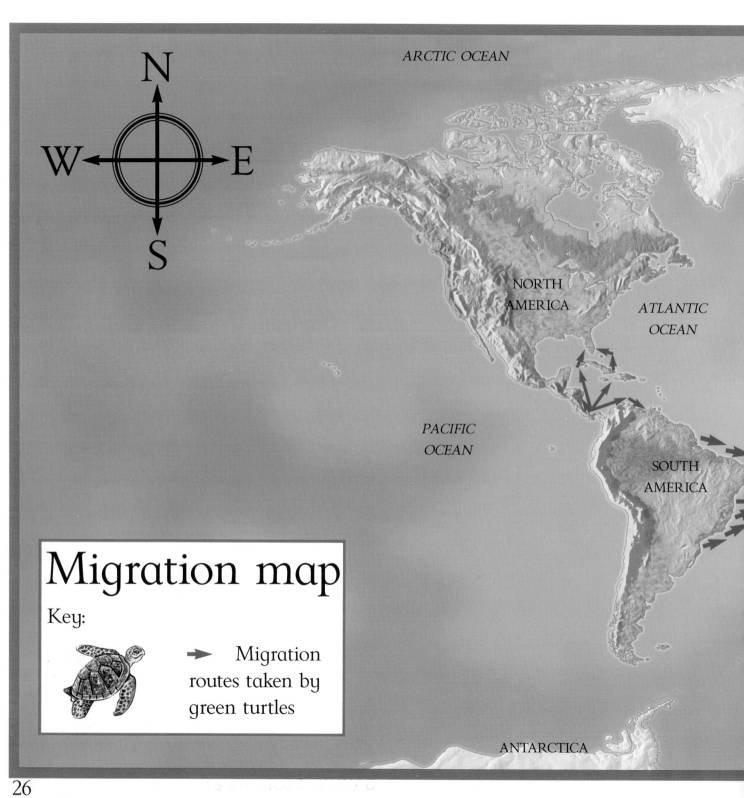

ARCTIC OCEAN

N

W E

S

NORTH
AMERICA

ATLANTIC
OCEAN

PACIFIC
OCEAN

SOUTH
AMERICA

Migration map

Key:

➤ Migration
routes taken by
green turtles

ANTARCTICA

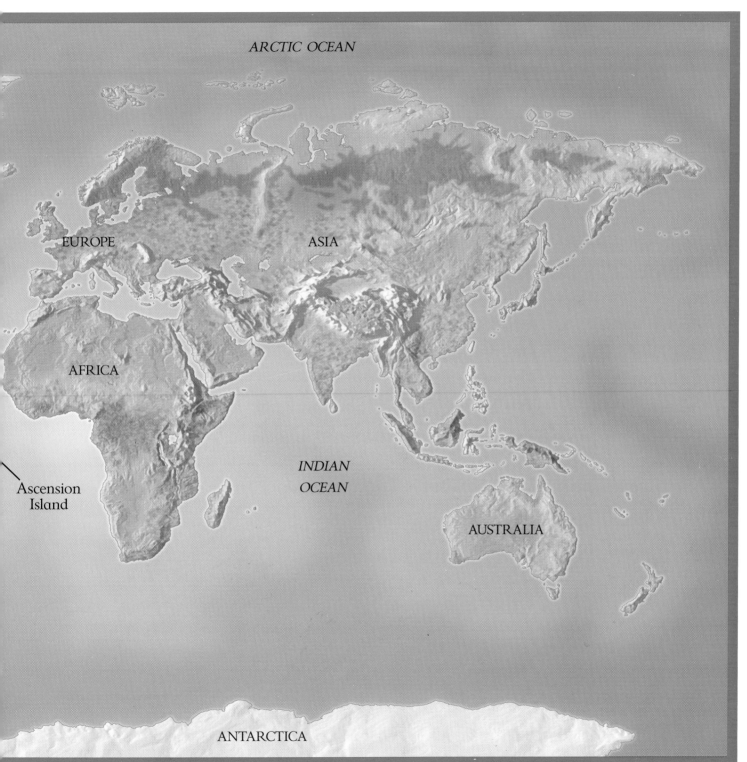

ARCTIC OCEAN

EUROPE

ASIA

AFRICA

INDIAN
OCEAN

Ascension
Island

AUSTRALIA

ANTARCTICA

Turtle words

Atlantic Ocean
The huge ocean between the east coast of America and the west coasts of Europe and Africa.

Clutch
The number of eggs laid by the female turtle.

Dawn
The time when the sun begins to rise at the beginning of the day.

Hatch
When the baby turtle breaks out of its eggshell.

Mating
When a mother (female) and a father (male) join to make babies.

Nesting chamber
The hole in the sand dug by the female turtle in which she lays her eggs.

Nightfall
When night comes and daylight ends.

Pacific Ocean
The largest and deepest of the world's oceans, stretching between the west coast of America and the eastern coast of South East Asia.

Shallow
Water that is not very deep. Turtles find most of their food in shallow water.

Shell
The hard covering of an egg which protects the growing baby turtle inside.

Survive
To live through a difficult or dangerous time, like the baby turtles who are not killed and eaten on their journey.

Index